Simon Cheshire

Series consultants:
Cliff Moon and Lorraine Petersen

nasen
NASEN House, 4/5 Amber Business Village, Amber Close,
Amington, Tamworth, Staffordshire B77 4RP

Rising Stars UK Ltd.
22 Grafton Street, London W1S 4EX
www.risingstars-uk.com

Published 2007

Cover design: Button plc
Illustrator: Pulsar Estudio (Beehive Illustration)
Text design and typesetting: Andy Wilson
Publisher: Gill Budgell
Commissioning editor: Catherine Baker
Editor: Clare Robertson
Series consultants: Cliff Moon and Lorraine Petersen

British Library Cataloguing in Publication Data.
A CIP record for this book is available from the British Library

ISBN: 978-1-84680-311-6

Printed by Craft Print International Limited, Singapore

Contents

Characters

Jon Commander of 2-Squad. He thinks he always knows best.

Laz Jon's second-in-command. He's used to following orders, not giving them.

Reth A soldier in 2-Squad. A coward, who can turn nasty when he's in danger.

Elza 2-Squad's radio officer. Not exactly her commander's biggest fan.

Pool The squad's prisoner. A lizard-like alien from a group called the Pellisar.

Narrator The narrator tells the story.

Scene 1

Trapped

Narrator It is the fourth century of the third calendar. Earth is at war. On the planet Pellison, the army of Earth is struggling. 2-Squad are cut off from their unit. Their enemies, the Pellisar, are firing at them. 2-Squad take shelter in a dark and dripping cave.

Jon Reth, tie up the prisoner!
Elza, try to contact our troop ship!
Laz, keep firing at the enemy!

Laz Aye, sir!

Elza Commander, if Laz
hits the rock above us …

Jon Are you in charge now, Elza?
Do as you're told!

Pool Releassse me! Let me go!

Reth You can behave too, mate.
I've had enough of you pelicans
for one day!

Pool We are called Pellisssar,
you human ssscum!

Reth Okay, pelican. Now shut up!

Narrator Laz fires laser bolts through
the mouth of the cave.
The sound bounces off the rocky walls.

Laz Got you! Sir, that was a direct hit
on a pelican war-car!
Six of them wiped out!

Jon Good shooting, lad.

Pool Oh no! My poor friends …

Reth Button it or you'll be next!
We've got to get off this planet.

Elza We're not going anywhere yet.
I can't get much of a signal in here.

Jon I told you to contact the ship!

Elza I'm doing all I can.
You led us in here, Commander!

Jon And you have the radio gear!
Do your job, soldier!

Laz I think the pelicans
are moving away, sir.
4-Squad must be leading them
to the mine.

Jon Hold your fire.
Stay low.

Elza At last, some sense.

Jon What did you say, Soldier?

Elza I said I'm getting some sense
out of the radio. Sir.

Jon Call for back-up.

Reth What? Not a rescue party?

Jon We've got a battle to win.

Reth I volunteer to take the prisoner
back to the ship. The boss
will want to question him.
If it *is* a him. Are you a him?

Pool Are *you*? All humansss look alike to me.

Jon You want a slap, pelican?

Pool I want my planet back.

Laz *Our* planet now. Right, sir?

Jon That's right, Laz, my boy.

Pool You're losing this war, human,
and you know it.
The Pellisssar will win.
We won't ressst until
every lassst human is sssent home.

Reth I really would belt up, mate.
Our commander won't like
what you're saying.

Jon I can't wait to hand you over
to the secret service boys.

Pool You would hand me over to my death.
Everyone knows how they treat
their prisonersss.

Jon We like to think of them
as firm, but fair.

Laz That's right.
We humans have standards.

Pool Humansss are evil.
You take our planet,
you take our minerals,
you take our food.

Reth We're just trying to survive.

Pool Ssso are we.
You've bled your own world dry,
and now you've come
to ruin oursss too.

Jon Earth has a mighty empire.
What's Pellison ever given
the universe?
The Pellisar nose flute!

Narrator As Jon, Reth and Laz laugh at their joke, Elza is listening to the noises on the radio.

Elza Quiet! I'm getting a link.

Narrator While the humans gather round the radio, Pool sees a chance to escape. He creeps towards the mouth of the cave, but …

Reth Oi!

Jon Get him!

Laz I've got it covered, sir!

Narrator Laz aims a laser blast above the alien's head.

Elza No! Don't blast the rock!

Narrator Too late. Laz fires.
The rock explodes, falling down
across the mouth of the cave.
The cave fills with dust.

Jon Get a light on in here!
It's pitch black.
Did Laz stop the prisoner escaping?

Pool I'm ssstill here, human.

Jon Well done, Laz.
You acted fast.
Not your fault about the rock.

Laz Thank you, sir.

Elza What? The man's an idiot!
I told him not to fire!
Now he's trapped us in here!

Reth She's right! Look!
The rocks have blocked
the mouth of the cave.
We're trapped!

Scene 2

The find

Narrator For many minutes, 2-Squad dig at the rock blocking the entrance to the cave.

Reth It's hopeless!
We're dead!
We're all dead!
And on this stupid little rock in space!

Jon Pack it in, Reth!
Elza, what about the radio?

Elza The signal's gone.
There's no way we can beam a message through all that rock.

Reth I knew it!
Dead! All of us!

Jon Shut up!

Reth The ship will think we've been wiped out in the battle. Nobody's going to come looking for us.

Pool I guessss the air in here
will be used up in about a day.
Maybe a day and a half at the most.

Elza Yes, you're right.
This cave is large,
but with five of us breathing …

Reth Then let's boost our chances.
I vote we kill the pelican.

Laz Me too. What do you say, sir?

Jon No matter how many of us there are,
we'll still run out of air in the end.
No, I say we dig. This ground is soft.
We can tunnel under the rock.

Elza But the rock is so heavy.
We have nothing we can use
to hold up the roof of a tunnel.

Jon Shall we just give up then?
Have you got a better idea?

Elza No, Commander.
I don't have a better idea.

Laz Then we dig!
Come on, all of you!
Time is against us.

Narrator The four humans and their
alien prisoner get to work.
But the digging is hard
and the cave is hot. It soon gets
hard to breathe.

Elza What's your name, Pellisar?

Pool My name isss Pool.
Of the Ninth Chapter of Pellison.

Elza I'm Elza.

Jon What on earth are you doing, soldier?

Elza We're all digging.
Aren't we on the same side now?

Laz You traitor!

Reth I've found something!
Hey, all of you, there's something under here.

Narrator	Reth and Laz dig a bit more, and pull out a box.
Laz	It's just some old pelican thing.
Elza	Those carvings on it are interesting. Pool, do they mean anything?
Pool	Let me sssee.
Narrator	The alien takes a close look at the box. Then he steps back, pale with fear.
Pool	It'sss a medicine box. Very old, maybe a thousand years. Do not open it!
Jon	Why? Something valuable inside? Gold? Money?
Laz	What's he hiding?
Pool	No! You don't undersssstand …

Reth I found it!
If there's gold inside, it's mine!
Right?

Pool Leave it alone!
It must have been buried for a reassson!

Elza Leave it!

Laz You really are a traitor, Elza!

Reth It should open up
if I just hit it on the top, I think.
There! It's open!
Bring the lamp over!

Laz What's inside?
What's in it?

Reth Nothing. Nothing at all.
It's empty.

Narrator The commander picks up the box
and smashes it to pieces.

Jon We're wasting time!
Get back to work.

Narrator They carry on digging.
But only a few minutes later,
Laz falls back, gasping.

Reth Laz? What's up?

Elza We're using up the air too fast.

Laz No, it's … I can't … Help me …

Jon What's wrong, lad?
What's that, on your face?

Reth Looks like a spider's web.
It's bright red and it's growing on him.

Pool Bloodfreeze.

Jon What did you say, pelican?

Pool It is the first sssign of Bloodfreeze.

Reth Tell me if I'm wrong here,
but the word 'bloodfreeze'
doesn't sound like good news.

Pool It is a diseassse, from long ago.
For years, it killed half the adults
of Pellissson, but we grew immune to it.
It's harmlessss to us now.

Reth To you? What about to us?
What about us humans?

Pool As you can sssee,
humans are not immune.
The box must have held living spores.
Deadly ssspores.

Elza There must be something we can do?
Anything?

Pool No. It took my people
hundreds of yearsss
to become immune to Bloodfreeze.

Jon The rest of you, dig! Fast!
We have to get Laz
to the medical bay on the ship.

Pool It isss too late.
Anyone who catches Bloodfreeze
isss dead within the hour.
And now that the ssspores
have been let out of the box,
you will all die.

Scene 3

Bloodfreeze

Narrator 2-Squad have fought in many battles. But this one looks as though it will be their last.

Elza He told us not to open that box! What's the matter with you lot? Is there mud where your brains should be?

Jon Shut up and dig!

Elza There's no way we can …

Narrator Suddenly, Elza falls to the ground.
The others hold up the lamp.
They see red, spidery lines
growing across her face.
The first sign of Bloodfreeze.

Reth She's got it too!
She's got it too!
Kill her! Kill her and Laz!
Stop it spreading.

Elza That's … what I like … about you,
Reth. You're always thinking of others.

Pool It will do no good to kill them.
The spores are in the air.

Laz Commander … Sir …
What's happened to the lamp?

Jon Nothing, lad. Why?

Laz It's gone out …
We're in the dark again.

Pool He's blind.

Jon Hold on, Laz.
We'll get you to the medics.

Reth No, we won't. It's hopeless.
We're all going to die,
just like the pelican said.

Jon I will not give in.
I will not let my squad be killed
by some filthy alien germ.
Reth, get back to digging!
And you, prisoner! Dig!

Elza My face feels numb.

Pool Please, ssstay ssstill.
The infection runs through the blood.
Can you humans
control your heartbeat?

Elza No, no we can't.

Pool Then it is very important
that you ssstay calm.

Jon Calm? Calm? Look at us!
This is your fault, alien!
Your fault!

Pool My fault? Why do humans
say such ssstupid things?

Narrator The commander and the Pellisar
begin to fight. Their hands
are locked around
each other's throats.
They kick up clouds of dust
from the floor of the cave.

Reth Commander! He's not worth the effort!
We've got enough to worry about.

Narrator The commander throws
Pool to the ground.
Pool crawls to the other side
of the cave.

Pool I know we are all afraid.
Even I am afraid.

Jon Speak for yourself!

Laz Commander!
I can't feel my legs!
It's in my legs now.
It's so hot in here.

Jon Hang on, boy.

Elza What … equipment …
do we have … between us?
Is there anything…
that can help us?

Pool I have an idea!

Narrator From the pack on his belt,
Pool takes a small machine.
It looks like a pocket calculator.

Pool This machine takes sssamples
from rocks, plants or animals.

Reth Great. We can have a hobby
before we die!

Elza Let him speak.

Pool We could take a sssample of my blood,
and one from you humans.
The machine may be able to change
the DNA in the human blood.

Elza You mean … make a cure?

Pool Not a cure, exactly.
The new blood would change
you forever. You would become
part-human, part-Pellisar.

Elza But the Bloodfreeze would stop?

Pool Yes.

Jon And you think we should do this?
Do you?

Laz Please … soon …
there's no time …

Pool I will give some of my blood
to sssave your lives.

Jon How big and brave of you!
Do you think I'm an idiot?
This is some sort of trick!
You pelicans are all the same.

Elza He's trying … to help us.

Jon How do you know?
He's got us in here, he's got us
breathing in his alien germs,
and now he's trying to make us
beg for his magic medicine!

Pool You must hurry.
I can't take a sssample
from a sssick human.
It must be from you or Reth.

Reth What? You've got to be joking!

Laz Save … us …
It's our only chance.

Elza We're fighting for our lives, Reth!

Reth This is war!
We're *all* fighting for our lives!

Jon You must think we're stupid, pelican.
You really think we're going to let you
turn us into aliens like you?

Pool You would live.

Jon We'd rather die.

Reth I wouldn't!
But I don't want to
turn half-lizard, either.

Jon We'd be selling out.
We are fighting this war
for the human empire –
not to poison ourselves
with alien blood!

Pool I see no other choice, human.
Either you die of Bloodfreeze,
or you become like me, and live.

Scene 4

Life and death

Narrator Laz and Elza are close to death.
The Bloodfreeze has crept
all through them now.

Reth I'll do it! Take my blood, alien!
I don't want to die!
Not like them!

Jon You little worm! Are you
with us or against us?
Will you be against us
when you turn half-lizard?

Reth I don't care.

Narrator Pool takes a sample of Reth's blood.
Moments later, the machine is ready.

Pool It has worked.
Now I need to inject each of you.

Laz Then do it! Quick!

Elza I'm blind too, now.
I'm scared. Pool, help us.

Jon What's the matter with you all?
We don't do deals with aliens!
We're at war with these pelicans!

Reth Well, one of these pelicans
is our only hope.

Narrator Pool injects Laz, Elza and Reth.
Jon refuses. He spits on the ground
at the alien's feet.

Pool That isss your choice, human.
Because you hate me, you will die.

Jon If I'm going to die,
I'll die human.

Narrator Suddenly, the three humans
who have been injected
begin to scream.
Their bodies twist, and then lie still.

Jon You've killed them!

Pool No. The DNA must have time to –

Jon I knew it! A trick!
You murderer!
I knew you weren't to be trusted!
You had to kill us all, before
we could escape this cave,
didn't you?
You pelicans must be wiped out!

Pool There isss no trick, human!

Jon Sorry, too late.

Narrator The commander pulls out his laser blaster. He aims and fires. Pool is knocked to the far side of the cave. He is dead before he hits the ground.

Jon I can feel it too, now. Bloodfreeze. I'm going to die, but at least I will die a real soldier. Not like these traitors.

Narrator Minutes pass. Laz, Elza and Reth slowly wake up.

Reth I'm alive! Alive! Unless I'm dead, and this is some sort of afterlife. Not much of an afterlife – it's the same cave I died in.

Elza You're alive, all right. We all are.

Laz It's amazing. The alien saved our lives.

Reth But not his own. Look!

Laz He's been laser-blasted!

Elza Poor Pool.
We treated him like scum,
and he still saved us.
Would we have done the same for him?

Laz Commander!

Reth Keep away from him!
He's got full-blown Bloodfreeze!

Elza We're immune to it now, idiot!

Jon Where are you?
I can't see you.

Laz We're alive, sir.
Thanks to the prisoner.

Elza Why did you kill him?

Jon I thought he'd tricked us.
I'm dying, Elza.
I can feel the Bloodfreeze.
I've never felt such pain.

Laz I'm proud to have worked
with you, sir.

Jon You don't mean that, lad.
You chose to side with the aliens.

Laz I made my own choice, for once.

Jon And I've made mine.
I choose to die.
I can't see any of you
but I bet you look like him.

Narrator With that, the commander of 2-Squad dies. Laz, Elza and Reth look at each other. Their faces have changed and they look part-alien now.

Laz What do we do?
How do we face our friends?
Our families?

Elza First, we get out of here.
We finish digging,
before the air runs out.

Reth Right! I'm not wasting a minute,
now I've got a whole new life.

Laz What if the army rejects us?
What if they treat us like the enemy?
And what if the Pellisar think the same?
Maybe the commander was right.
Maybe we should have chosen death.

Elza What if there are more boxes
like that out there?
What if more humans
have to do what we've done?

Reth I think we should hide.
On a moon somewhere
that is nice and quiet.
Let this whole war thing blow over.

Elza No. Like you said, we've got
a whole new life now.
We'll have a whole new war
on our hands, once we get out there.

Laz What's going to happen to us?

Elza I don't know, soldier. I don't know.

Narrator They get to work, digging a tunnel.
After many hours, they crawl
to freedom. Soon afterwards,
the tunnel collapses behind them.
The commander is left inside the cave
for all time, along with the alien
who tried to save him.

Drama ideas

1

After Scene 1

- With a partner, pretend to be Elza and Jon.
- Jon thinks that Elza should show more respect, but Elza doesn't think Jon listens to his crew enough. Act out an argument between the two characters.

After Scene 2

2

- Hotseating: Choose one person to be Pool.
- Everyone else can ask Pool questions, e.g. how does it feel to be a prisoner of the enemy? Does he like some members of 2-Squad better than others?

After Scene 3

- In your group, act out the end of the scene, from where Pool offers to give his blood to the humans.
- Freeze at the end of the scene.
- Each character can take turns to say what they are thinking.

After Scene 4

- In your group, each choose one of the characters still alive at the end of the play. How do they feel about the future?
- Take on the role of your character and tell the rest of the group your hopes and fears.

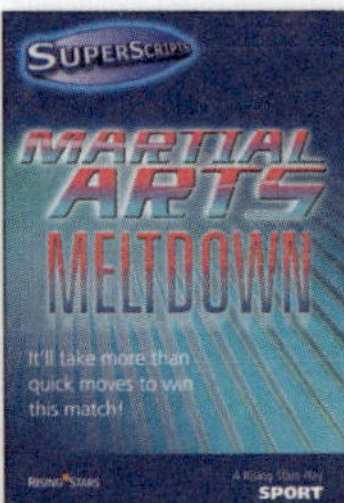

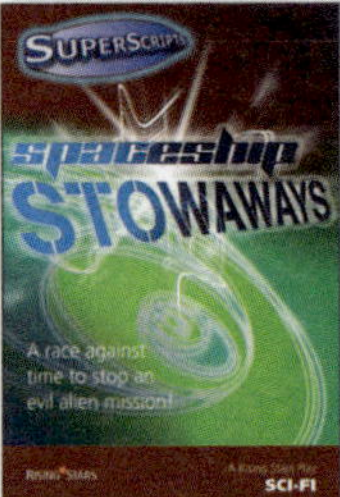

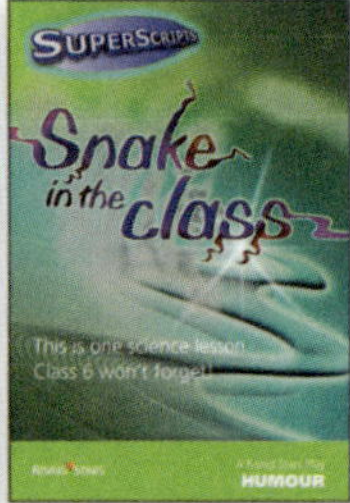

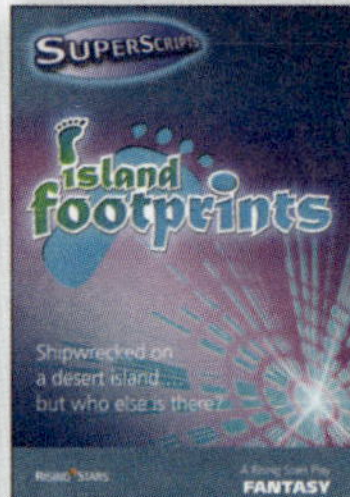

PHONE

0871 47 23 010

www.risingstars-uk.com